Selected Poems

Selected Poems
Archie Minasian

Introduction by William Saroyan

Afterword by Aram Saroyan

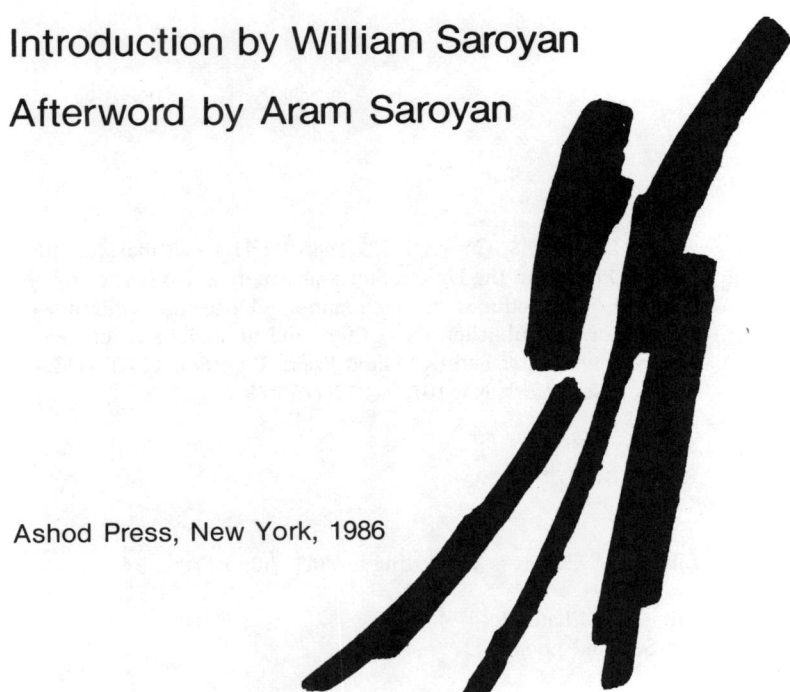

Ashod Press, New York, 1986

SELECTED POEMS. Copyright © 1986 by Helen Minasian. All rights reserved. Printed in the United States of America. No part of this book may be used or reproduced in any manner whatsoever without written permission of the publisher, except for brief quotations embodied in articles and reviews. Published by Ashod Press, P.O. Box 1147, Madison Square Station, New York NY 10159. 212/475/0711.

FIRST EDITION

Library of Congress Cataloging-in-Publication Data

Minasian, Khatchik.
    Selected poems.

    I. Title.
PS3563 . I463A6   1986   811'. 54   86-10751
ISBN 0-935102-18-3

Contents

Introduction by William Saroyan   7

PART I / The Simple Songs   9

The Snow   11
Valley Ditch   12
Rule 449   13
The Little Feet   14
The Cure   15
Becoming Great   16
An Evening at Home   17
How Foolish the Sweating Men   18
They Bring Me Raisins   19
Parlor Talk   20
The Holy War   20
The Workers   21
Afternoons and Evenings   22
The Poplar   23
Memories of My Father   23
Water Light   24
A Romp with the Wind   24
The Message   25
Tiger Wind   26
Old Things   26
Seasonal Submission   27
A Bald Prospect   28
Night Does That   29

PART II / My Tiny Dynasty (A Prose Interlude)   31

PART III / Beyond the Gage (Later Poems)   39

Escape   41
My Cohort   42

In the Memory   43
Beyond the Gage   44
The Lily   45
Crossing a Street   45
Apparitions on the Wall   46
Prints   48
Early Summer through Los Banos   49
Dreams and Desires   50
Contrasts   51
Extremes   52
Kinship   53
Unwary Youth   54
Farewell to Willie   55
Night Interlude   56
Reflections   57
My Song   58
The Inner Joys   59

Afterword by Aram Saroyan   61

INTRODUCTION

The feeling in the use of language by Khatchik Minasian seems to me to be Asiatic. He says very old things in a very few number of words. Beyond the words one feels the impact of a great deal of wisdom which may be unconscious—that is to say, inevitable rather than deliberate. It is an Asiatic wisdom, I feel, in that there is little or no protest in it. The design of a poem seems startling in its simplicity. The poem is an arrangement of odds and ends into something immediately fresh, although the objects forming the arrangement are old and often commonplace. This is good art for besides the specific arrangement and the pleasure it gives is the inescapable suggestion of many more similar arrangements for the reader to establish for himself. In short, his poems evoke out of the reader's experience a great deal that is rare that would not come to body without the push of Minasian's own poetic energy.

The absence of protest in this poetry is a virtue, for protest is a new and unproved idea in the art of poetry, and if encouraged might conceivably lead any clear-thinking poet to a justified protest against poetry itself. If the poet is to find fault in anything, sooner or later he must find fault in everything, for fault is surely there; and to find fault in everything is to roam the world and come home to find fault in the poet himself; and then, no doubt, to find fault in finding fault, which brings the poet with an Asiatic spirit right into the heart of his life and business, which is a business of knowing and not caring to find fault. It is a poetry that brings rest to hardworking and eager spirits. The reader will find Khatchik Minasian's poetry smiling rather than laughing.

How it came to pass that Mr. Minasian's use of English in the writing of poetry is Asiatic is one of those simultaneously over-simple and extra-complex matters which grows more troublesome the more one attempts to figure it out; consequently I shall not try to figure it out. The situation pleases me and that's quite enough, I think. He writes what he writes as no one else in America could write it. Surely some of this uniqueness is the result of ignorance on his part, but ignorance, it must be understood, is more often a valuable element of a poet's equipment than a handicap. The man who knows all about poetry is seldom the man who writes poetry. The man who writes poetry seldom knows a great deal about it.

I do not gather from having often read the poems in this collection that Mr. Minasian has studied the great writers of modern poetry. And I do not gather that he has studied the great writers of ancient poetry. What appears to have happened is that he wanted to write a poem one day and one day did so. That is probably how poetry began in the first place. If a pretty good man is involved it would appear to be just about the best way to get poetry. As I understand things a pretty good man would be one who knows his own insignificance and yet has an inexhaustible pride; a man who is infinitely careless and yet takes a lifetime to get a detail right; a man who lives much better than his writing about it and yet at the right moment writes better about it than any man could ever live.

I could never know for sure, but my hunch is that Khatchik Minasian is, or is by way of becoming, such a man. It takes time of course. It takes time every time a man thinks he is ready to get some poetry. It takes a century or so even at that very moment. And I believe the reader will recognize in reading these poems that each of them has come forward out of a great deal of this taking of time. In my opinion Khatchik Minasian is a poet. This modest volume is apt to be the first part of a long wonderful poem.

1950   *William Saroyan*

PART I

The Simple Songs

THE SNOW

When winds begin to rouse the idle leaves,
    and night falls in,
And little bodies quit their favorite spot—
Reluctant till the morrow turns them out,
    I tip-toe in—
        enchanter of the night,
        the child's delight.

Through meadows wide and little hidden yards
    I spread my charm
And turn all blemishes of land to one
Expanse of Nature's purest finery.
    With no alarm
        the gentle wood and field
        to me do yield.

Impatient till the morn, I shall expect
    some child to meet—
My first sweet blemish that shall mar my grace,
Some half-awakened eye in wild surprise;
    and then the feet
        that I shall kiss in haste
        though it me waste.

Valley Ditch

In our ditch
      there are water skaters,
      frogs,
      tall reeds,
      mud bugs,
      apple cores and plum seeds,

      and little naked children.

Rule 449

boy with blackspider
on hat,
and four June bugs
on new red sweater,
parades before student body
holding bull-frog high.

principal summons boy
to office,
begins with rule 173—
(not to molest fellow student)
        eye on spider;
ends with rule 449—
(becomes property of school)
        hand on bull-frog.

The Little Feet

We mark a patch of early snow
with little feet
quite deep and neat.

There's not a place we wish to go
with sheets of chill
upon a hill.

There's not a care our steps will show
in any track
you follow back.

There's not a thing we wish to know
with little feet
quite deep and neat.

THE CURE

Restless
I pace my little room,
swing the windows and look out.

The trees on the hill are tossing madly;
I watch them,
I am thrilled at their madness.

I turn to my bare room satisfied.

Becoming Great

We look at Goethe
           and Schiller,
huge bronze statues
           in the park,

and we think,
someday we'll be like them—
           you Goethe and I Schiller.

Then through narrow park lanes
           we crawl along,
           solemn and confident,
           eloquent and witty,
ignoring the boys that pass on bicycles
and the girls in shorts
           carrying tennis rackets.

An Evening at Home

The guests are seated in the evening parlor
smoking Izmir tobacco;
they are pleased.
The children will have dried figs
and candied nuts.
Suddenly a guest is praised for her gifted voice;
dragged to the piano
by the bearded aunt,
she giggles and cannot sing.
Excitement wears to silence;
the hostess serves coffee
in the new gift cups;
the parlor becomes a tavern,
there is smoke and noise,
the sleepy children are bored,
they drift into various rooms.

The guests must go,
the children nod and fret,
and then commotion in the house
as hat and wrapper hunts begin.
Farewells are shouted and exchanged,
but wait! the guests will take dried figs
and candied nuts with them.

Another pause, another word or two,
another dip of Izmir for the pipes.

They go at last,
they know the way.

How Foolish the Sweating Men

Ha for a long review of everything
now that old Summer plans to leave.

How comforting the fields we pass
with the slanting hay;

How pure the air we breathe
and our thoughts;

How inviting the lushy meadows,
the wandering girls by roadsides;

How jubilant each hedge
with the bird;

How dear the farmhouse half hidden
with gardens adjoining and vines sloping;

How cool the broad canal
and the lanky weeds and the weir;

How distant the brown bare hills,
the solitary trees;

How still the air,
how dense the views we pass;

How foolish the men sweating in orchards,
shaking the peach and the last ripe plum.

They Bring Me Raisins

We sit, and gazing on the hills
   my thoughts go wild.
I see the road that led me to
   her house in snow,
and autumn just begun,
I cannot bear the long months in my mind,
   or push the drift.

They bring me raisins, figs and dates,
and press me to the wine.
They see my father in my face
   and ask of home;
I give strange answers.

Parlor Talk

The guests sat on the new sofa,
they talked of old things;
we sat on old chairs
and talked of new things.

They talked of new things and grew old;
We talked of old things and dashed out.

The Holy War

We go to the meadow,
    a small army.
We are going to gather mushrooms
    and fire wood.
      We carry spade and axe
    and gunny sacks.

Nothing will stop us.

The Workers

In my presence
the men work feverishly at their tasks,
      denying themselves tobacco
and conversation.

In my absence,
      like air bags expiring,
      they sink to comfortable places
and roll cigarettes
      and discuss cheap labor.

Afternoons and Evenings

Hazy afternoons
    and workers on the grass reclining,
    ignoring the crops
    and the strong sun on their faces.

Cool evenings
    and witty city girls
    taking advantage
    of farm boys.

The Poplar

The rain brings Autumn's last leaf down,
Relief! the poplar cries, relief!

The snow enwraps the naked bough,
The leaf! the poplar cries, the leaf!

Memories of My Father

the wind spoke to me
I went to the orchard,
leaves came down
        of every kind
with busy whisperings
I could not understand.

Water Light

It is night,
>and on the river
>lights, like banners, hang from every boat;
>and to the shore
>they join the puddles where I stand.

I watch them play in the eddies
>>and go on.

A Romp with the Wind

The wind threw rose petals at me,
tugged my hair
>and pushed me around.

Flattered,
I ran with the wind
>and called it names.

THE MESSAGE

Though I go my way calmly,
humble in countenance,
know, my love,
my soul is loud with rebuke,
my mien restrained,
my desire fierce.

Tiger Wind

The wind,
playing in the violets,
sprang upon me.

Oh! I thought,
if I could be so familiar
with her.

Old Things

These are old leaves,
    do not disturb them.

The wind is shaking olives down.

These are old thoughts,
    do not destroy them.

She is wearing out my heart.

Seasonal Submission

The autumn wind,
like a maddened officer,
fell upon our trees,
    jerking the leaves from their sockets.

I watch him recruiting them
for sky service.

A Bald Prospect

In our youth
neighbor Sanasar and I
passed for twins.

Now that time has passed,
I wonder if we haven't taken
too long to discover
there's not a hair of truth
between us.

Night Does That

We camp along rivers
in new canvas beds;

we are six
at night.

John plays the harmonica
with both hands—

about lovers
and sentimental things.

We crawl away
to dark places and listen;

John plays his best
by the fire, alone;

we know he is sad
when he plays softly—

about lovers
and sentimental things;

and he knows
we are smoking cheap tobacco

in dark places,
thinking.

PART II

My Tiny Dynasty

A Prose Interlude

MY TINY DYNASTY

Shall I tell you about my family, my wife and six children? Of course! How delightfully unique, at least I think they are, having to bear up under my old fashioned eye, patriarchal in a sense, barking around the house to establish this order. But the home is special to us, as I am sure it is to so many, many others; to maintain this standard, I find we must work at it tirelessly, with few personal pleasures: no parties, solo trips, social gatherings, etc. At this point, it should be obvious that the children are never left alone. True! A drab existence?—nonsense! We are never bored, angry at times and violently alive tending to the needs of our own. They have all learned to sew, to cook, wash, bake, prepare a table—and play, and all of this with a sense of competition and fun.

My purpose is to prolong childhood as long as possible, stretching this delightful age of fantasy and purity to its very limits. To do this, I have found it necessary to shut out some of the outside current. The burden of course falls heavily on the mother. I supply the stout voice and direction and she the patience, love and labor. Thus the family unit remains, woven about it something rich and meaningful. How rewarding, how pure, almost god-like. The children are safe under the watchful eye and that is all important to us.

As I said, I have six children, five girls and a boy. Frances, the eldest, has remained timidly gentle, almost reserved, perhaps because she has had to listen to my roars over a longer period of time. Lolly is smart and confident, at times the tease; Roxanne serene and proud; Diane brooding and wise, and, often to the extreme, hysterically gigglish; Ellen is mischievously happy; and Vahan, the boy, seems molded with a dash of each, amused by the turbulence of five feminine personalities. And my yelling only arouses his little frame to a curious excitement, a necessary performance, the manly function of all fathers. He smiles shyly, and this I accept as an approval. All together, very gratifying, daughters, son, noise and all.

Since I rarely allow the children to play outdoors, much to the annoyance of the neighbors, the house is used for a playground.

"Don't run!" I shout.

"Do you have to yell?"

"Why do they gallop? They'll break their necks going through the hallway."

"What else can they do?"

"They can walk, that's what."

"Then please don't yell. Listen to your father, girls!"

"Let them color books or read awhile."

"That's all they do."

"Too bad. Shall I turn them out into the streets? It's the easy way."

"Darn you."

I go out and return almost at once. The girls, all banded together, smile.

"What's wrong?"

"Nothing."

"You look like conspirators. Let's have it!"

Roxanne shows me the paper. There is a cartoon festival at the local theatre. "That's out!" I yell. They giggle, then lining abreast, begin a stand of lovely pouting. "Cut it out!"

"It won't hurt you to go out for a change," my wife interjects.

"Is that so! I suppose you are all crucified." I take the paper and smile. The children let out with a cheer, and to make it final, sing out: "Who's the sweetest man in town? Daddy! Daddy!" I submit, crushed and delighted. * * *

I am really a gentle man in spite of my rough exterior, of medium height, possessed with some physical strength. I go out of my way to be helpful and am considered a good family man. To my immediate neighbors however, those who live within ear-shot and catch the thundering outbursts, I am an enigma. They run for cover on occasions and come forth at times like dear lost friends. There are the children of course who keep me in a state of frenzy and buoyancy, levelling me at every turn.

I became a painter (I paint for a living) quite by accident; one could say I forced it on myself unknowingly, for I had other plans and had gone a comfortable distance towards achieving my purpose. I had studied the natural sciences, and the poets (having written several books of poetry), and decided on entomology, the study of insects. I was fond of these winged ones and felt almost a kinship for their tribes, the burrowers, flitters, buzzers, crawlers, loafers, sleepers—tribes worth knowing. The sight of a beetle produced a certain delightful glow, the desire to pause and probe, to greet and converse (I have conversed with dragon-flies), a hungry want, an urge to understand this prodder of the earth, the same desire one gets when meeting a lost friend, and clasping arms sits to chat with that impatient joy of sincere fellowship.

I volunteered to help a friend with his house, worked so swiftly with the brush, with the natural feel as they say, that others took note and made offers, which in turn mounted gradually into some running business. It seemed profitable at the time, and there was some contentment in achieving a craft so easily come by, but before I had had time to appraise my direction, found the road well marked, my former path pitifully erased (for there were those who felt that I had found my natural calling with the insects).

* * *

How often I have sat up in the dark, in the dead night where everything seems frightfully empty and real, when all errors gather about in a mental gallery and demand reappraisal. And in my review, moments of delicious joy and quiet, nothing but truth and time to contemplate it. Crazy human race, I think.

And how often (after outbursts) I have felt ashamed and angry with myself, wanting to go in to the children and talk with them, quietly, to make up for all the harsh words so thoughtlessly said, the threats and violent demonstrations that had frightened them so often. I want to tell them how sorry I am, that I only meant the best, even when I was raving like a madman. Instead, I get out of bed and go into the patio and take in the cool mold-scented air. The night air revives me and I stiffen lion-like, daring the world to interfere with my own little universe. I go in and survey my small domain. All I find is peaceful slumber. And there is my wife. Poor woman, I think, children and confinement. Then stalking the rooms like a thief, I shrivel a bit, cover the helpless slumberers, flex my muscles in a sign of thanks and retire.

The house is still today, save for the kitchen. The door is closed, but inside there is noise and merriment. I know they are baking, the weird shapes taking form, some flat, some puffed, some glazed, some sugared, all somehow delicious and new in design. The wholesome odors rise up and invade the neighborhood. I can hear the children at the back door, receiving samples my girls are passing out. How delightful.

I walk in later and explode just to explode; something must be wrong. Watch the cutters! not too close, back, back! Not so much flour. Did you wash your hands? Not on the floor—easy! I weary in moments (for no one has heard a thing I've said) and retire to the patio where coffee and the new kitchen dandies are rushed for testing. I protest, about the weight I'm putting on from the hot pastry, but manage to empty a tray.

I sneak around the back and stand admiring my crew through the window. Bless them all; they've been at it all day. The hour is late and they are at it in full force, laughter and spirit, as if the day had just begun. And tomorrow, in the sewing room, I know I shall be shouting, crushing their spirit a bit, but only for a while. But surely this must sharpen them, I think.

Tonight I shall walk the floor again like a haunted man, in the dark, through the rooms, reflecting, wondering, muttering, chained to my conscience like a beast. In the dead of night, how absurd it all seems—my uncontrollable fury, my discipline, the noise, demands, restrictions, regrets . . . and why must I tip-toe about like a thief and listen at the doors to the children breathing, listen and shrivel at the soul? Why do my punishments always backfire?

* * *

How quickly the new day has begun. The house hums again. The machine whirrs, scissors snip and colored material pieces fall about the rooms. Since all final decisions are mine, I am called on only too frequently to judge—condemn or approve.

The dress is ready for hemming. Call Daddy. I enter, grumbling.

"Up a little—lower!"

"I don't want it so long."

"Just let me decide."

Frances is on the verge of tears.

"Relax!" I bark. "Don't try to look like everyone else. Be different."

My wife seems concerned, for there are many to be managed.

"It could go up a little," she whispers fearfully.

"Let me do the thinking around here."

And so my judgment carries through again.

"By the way, where is Vahan?" I ask.

He emerges smiling. He has several costumes for his rubber pig. I can't help laughing. He grins and disappears, and soon the sewing machine is whirring again. "Him too?" I ask bewildered. "That's enough!" I yell to him. "Go in the back and play."

The work is over, the children scatter. Then suddenly the door bell rings and they are back in a flash, full of expectancy. A voice calls through the door: "Can Ellen play?"

"Not today," I shout. "Some other time."

"And when is that?" my wife asks.

"Never mind! If one goes out, that's it . . . the house falls down."

* * *

When the children come in and kiss my cheek (they always do before going to bed), I want to reach out and hug them; but imagine, I am embarrassed.

Time for reflection? . . . naturally. What divine moments, brief, essential, pure, and I am at it in full force. I notice things about my patio each day, things that somehow weren't there the day before, or a moment ago—the way the heavy eaves jut awkwardly from the roof, the tiny patch of grass (our lawn) no bigger than a picnic table, and the way the house stands pitifully against it, everything here in my life, marked off in paces, an infinitesimal island and I the master. Master, imagine. I am hardly able to manage myself.

37

Tomorrow I shall drive the children to the hills. Somehow they have learned of this for they are already shouting with glee, dashing through the rooms and leaping about from the glad shock. What else can I do? I must carry through with my thoughts.

I sit back and reflect nobly, pleased and flushed with inner joy, and in my reverie, my own words come to me:

> Peaceful is my house among the trees
> and the wind is calm,
> peaceful sits my love in the garden
> of my mind,
> she speaks kind messages to me;
> the names I called her
> I have all withdrawn.

PART III

Beyond the Gage

Later Poems

Escape

I shall go to the high mountains
before the thaw,
when rivers are low
and the ice hangs from every drip and fall.

I shall cross the deep snow
in the tall timber
above the keeper's watch
to the barest crags beyond,
to the treacherous heights
the chamois fears.

Even you, my love,
shall not dissuade me.

My Cohort

The summer night is enchanting;
I wish to shout and sing,
clap my hands instead
and breathe deeply.

One tiny frog
in the marsh thicket
however
expresses my pure joy.

In the Memory

A man once turned a mad dog
    on a crowd of us—
    all unsuspecting boys;

he came to me,
    as if I stood alone
    to challenge his fierce sanity;

but in my moment of despair
    the beast seemed shyly put
    as though he understood,

remembering it seemed
    a similar assault
    his own mind had withstood.

Beyond the Gage

We probed the universe
on the heights of Aragats,
made positive identifications
in the light-year zone,
viewed Uranus calmly
as if a tempting plum
just overhead,
closed the session smartly with a gay huzza
and started down the heights
when suddenly a wall of hieroglyphics
tumbled out of the centuries
and confounded us all.

The Lily

The night lily,
heavy in the damp air,
revealed a mood
I had forgotten,

so many images
and back so suddenly.

Crossing a Street

If you ever cross a street
and say hello
to everyone you meet,
what difference if you've never met.

And yet I sense
occasional surprise,
as if I stole a salutation
meant for other eyes.

Apparitions on the Wall

Ache Armenian heart,
there's Ararat.

From the walls
the joy, the pride, the pain
that sustains.

Shall I hail our Kings and Queens
and Patriarchs,
or ask, how fled the years,
the wasted golden days
when pride and envy
dispersed the ancient founts?
and shall I ask,
what thoughts brood frozen in the head?

And all you infant sons
in borrowed rags,
like play-time warriors
assembled for a glory out of reach,
children meant for better things—
with eyes of resignation and despair
as if betrayed.
Hail!

And hail to the faces
lost upon the walls,
the noble hearts exposed
with all their hopes left in to dry.

And to you, hail!
spokesman for them all,
whose every note a requiem sounds.
Sing Shah Mourad! Arouse! Remind!
appease the apparitions on the wall!
inflame the heart again!

Prints

What a clutter man has left behind,
and mine I place beside
the margin of the road;
and here an incomparable design
clean set,
signifying a burden of its own.

Early Summer through Los Banos

From off the fields
abstract designs in crazy patterns
appear and assemble
like an instant gallery
in greens and mustard-yellow.

Two eyes,
two legs, two wings,
a twisted head,
and suddenly a burst,
like mushy grapes or tinted snow,
life instantly immobilized
and lost forever.

No lengthy summer sun,
no wide expanse to flit across,
no promise of a winged destiny—
fulfillment of a frenzied afternoon,
relinquished all to progress of the road
and mounted in some grotesque bas-relief.

Dreams and Desires

Oh to be caught in some magical spell
where fancy soars
and the spirit, wildly free,
a whirling demon leaps.

Out, out
like the hawk-eye soaring
in swift survey
with vibrant exhilaration,
free, direct and unerring,

soaring, soaring
and back a predator,
full of the hunt and satisfied.

Contrasts

I met an old man grimly
hurrying through life
in pursuit of the unattainable;

and there a youth sat idly by
in the early summer sun
trading shadows with his years.

EXTREMES

Even in my darkest thoughts
my foolish heart describes the Spring
as if I was prepared for such things.

KINSHIP

1.

How well that voice
I hear
coming from the small brook
tells my own story.

2.

Though I search
the bottomless pool in vain,
what I seek
I know is there.

Unwary Youth

Remember me, capricious Muse,
unwary youth on Fresno street,
fool enough to chance a ride
when you appeared and picked me up
and barbed me like a summer plum?

How long I've spiralled through the skies
and dipped and melted out of sight,
jostled by your crazy moods,
a captive anchored to your side
like Ahab to his whale.

Farewell to Willie

The birds are in his trees
among the leaves
feeding on the early plum and peach.

Soon they will be off
in the morning sky
and he will be with them.

Night Interlude

In the deep night
a dove coo'd
its pure sorrow

and almost at once
the mockingbird
answered in a shameless
burst of frivolous chatter,
as if it meant to say as much.

Embarrassed,
the deep night
held its breath.

Reflections

She was designed of gentle things
and he of black attire,
together on a hill they viewed
the glow of human fire.

The masses in the valley grew,
the tumult and the light,
she saw a world of promises
and he eternal night.

And as they marked the timeless span
and charted what to tell,
he thought he caught a glimpse of hope
and she a shade of hell.

My Song

The voice is like a laughing brook,
    it chatters all day long,
it sings of this and sings of that,
    I liken it to song.

The song is summertime, it's rain,
    beginning and began,
a ceaseless gushing through the earth
    and through the stream of man.

It leaps the rock, and under grass
    flows sweetly on its way,
to each articulating heart
    a merry roundelay.

The voice is like a laughing brook,
    it chatters all day long,
it sings of this and sings of that,
    I liken it to song.

The Inner Joys

While my friends sought the glitter,
I followed the inner joys,
tramping the gardens and the wilds
in harmony with nature.
I bared my soul
and sought in return
the ways of her infinite mysteries
that nourished my questionings and desires.

I sought and was nurtured,
I to her giving and she to my quest.

I found in time that we were one,
exposed to an abiding law.

When the winds of Time arrived
and swept the weary fields and woods,
and called on all things to submit,
I too as one in harmony,
touched by the icy couriers,
knew my quest had been fulfilled
and naught remained but summoning.

"Prepare thy hearth," I thought,
"for what has been
shall surely be again
for he who cares to seek this room."

Afterword

F. Scott Fitzgerald remarks somewhere that the poet's talent matures early, while the novelist's best work is likely to come later on in life. Although Archie Minasian wrote several plays and a novel, he was preeminently a poet, and the poems in his first collection, *The Simple Songs of Khatchik Minasian* (The Grabhorn Press, San Francisco, 1950), establish so high a standard that if he hadn't written another word, his position as one of the remarkable literary artists of his generation would, I think, still be secure.

These are unmistakably American poems, but an older culture hovers and broods over them. Minasian's intimate domestic scenes—his portraits of young lovers constrained in the parlors of their elders—are winking cameos of an age-old drama. In "They Bring Me Raisins," for instance, the lovesick young narrator is forced to endure the questions of his elders:

> They bring me raisins, figs and dates,
> and press me to the wine.
> They see my father in my face
>   and ask of home;
> I give strange answers.

But Minasian, the social miniaturist, never settles for social commentary alone. Rather he makes each player in the drama a part of a mosaic, and when the design is seen whole, a sense of the universal seems at once to permeate these wittily observed scenes from the provinces.

If Minasian excels at his sort of old world-new world comedy of manners, it is as a nature poet, I would venture, that he reached his greatest heights. From the first poem in *The Simple Songs,* in which he anthropomorphizes snow, we are in the presence of a sensibility in the most intimate and delighted interaction with the forces of the natural world:

>With no alarm
>>the gentle wood and field
>>to me do yield.
>
>* * *
>
>Some half awakened eye in wild surprise;
>>and then the feet
>>>that I shall kiss in haste
>>>though it me waste.
>
>("The Snow")

As these two excerpts indicate, from the beginning the poet had a penchant for pointing up a pattern in the natural world that suggests a parallel in human terms. Sometimes he will make this parallel explicit, as in "Tiger Wind":

>The wind,
>playing in the violets,
>sprang upon me.
>
>Oh! I thought,
>if I could be so familiar
>with her.

In another instance, one world will answer directly to the needs of the other, as in "My Cohort," one of Minasian's later lyrics:

>The summer night is enchanting;
>I wish to shout and sing,
>clap my hands instead
>and breathe deeply.

> One tiny frog
> in the marsh thicket
> however
> expresses my pure joy.

By the time of "The Inner Joys," one of the major poems of Minasian's later period, this penchant seems to have yielded a sense of a large current of experience common to both the human world and the world of nature. Speaking of nature in this poem, the narrator says: "I found in time that we were one, / exposed to an abiding law."

This isn't the vision of Minasian's fellow Californian and poet elder, Robinson Jeffers, who saw the universe in terms of its majestic, chilling indifference, but neither is it that "enervated transcendentalism" of the genteel tradition that reduced nature to a middle class accessory, men and women, as Santayana saw it, thinking "themselves in the throes of some rapturous interpenetration of mind and nature—when they were doing little else than taking the air." Minasian may have often and freely anthropomorphized nature, but he never trivialized it. In the moving final two stanzas of "The Inner Joys," the narrator speaks of the end of his life:

> When the winds of Time arrived
> and swept the weary fields and woods,
> and called on all things to submit,
> I too as one in harmony,
> touched by the icy couriers,
> knew my quest had been fulfilled
> and naught remained but summoning.
>
> "Prepare thy hearth," I thought,
> "for what has been
> shall surely be again
> for he who cares to seek this room."

The sense of continuance with which the poem closes, a sense arrived at through the poet's consciousness of the natural, seasonal cycles of death and rebirth, is something Minasian shares with both Gary Snyder and Lew Welch, two younger California poets who trace their poetic roots back to classical Chinese nature poetry and to whom he is closer in spirit than he is to Jeffers. For these poets, awareness of nature has yielded what might be called an enlarged humanism, one that looks from the confines of the room out into the fields and mountains and sky—often to find there a kind of healing. It is to just this lively and enduring tradition, it seems to me, that Archie Minasian brought his unique elegance, wit, and depth of feeling.

Aram Saroyan